I COULDN'T CATCH THE BUS TODAY

I Couldn't Catch The Bus Today

The true story of a nervous breakdown
that became a pilgrimage

DAVID LAZELL

LUTTERWORTH PRESS
GUILDFORD AND LONDON

First Published 1973

ISBN 0 7188 2072 X
Copyright © 1973 David Lazell

*Printed in Great Britain
by Cox and Wyman Ltd, London, Reading and Fakenham*

This book is dedicated as a thank you to those who care for the mentally ill and anxious, in and out of hospital; to Mrs Alice Neville of The Open Door fellowship; and to my wife, Anne, who has had to live with my problems. I hope that my experiences will 'open that door' to those who suffer from agoraphobia and anxiety states.

CONTENTS

ABOUT THIS BOOK

This book seeks to record the experience of one man who suffered a nervous breakdown in the summer of 1972. The man – David Lazell – had suffered from agoraphobia (fear of open spaces) for some twenty-five years, and only went into mental hospital as a last resort. Although he was not to be cured, he found so much spiritual insight at the hospital that he now considers his stay 'perhaps the most important month of my entire life'. He has recorded his impressions in a lively way to help those who suffer from anxiety, as well as to aid ministers who have to consider how they may best help the anxious in their congregations. In order to avoid any embarrassment, the author had changed names and locations in some of the cases mentioned in this book, but the material is based on fact, and also reflects the author's views on ministry today.

'I gained a better picture of God through the people that I met' . . . those encounters are described in this book.

I

Arrival

The mental hospital was at the end of a deserted country road. I gazed out of the taxi windows at the staff houses clustered together at the entrance. The swish-swish of the car's windscreen wipers made a melancholy background to my thoughts.

Through the rain that fell so heavily that morning, I tried to read the various direction signs. We turned up a tree-lined avenue. Birds – so similar to those I knew in my garden at home – hopped cheekily across the lawns. Even on that dismal morning, one could not but notice the beautiful flowers in the hospital gardens.

'Which house is it, sir?' The taxi driver, a cheerful man, appeared momentarily lost.

Anne looked at the admission form.

'Harvey. Anne – my wife, who had live through my 'nervous ups and downs' for our fourteen years of marriage – squeezed my hand. I did not feel at all like entering a mental hospital, not even one as attractive as this.

'Here we are, sir.' The taxi stopped, and the driver began to collect the cases from the boot. Bewildered and discouraged, I followed my wife from the car. Harvey House – a large red brick building – seemed deserted, and there were no instructions apparent to guide new patients. Overcome by an attack of panic (common enough in anxiety states) I suggested getting back into the taxi and returning home. The driver looked a little concerned. Anne took command of events, and we found another entrance which led to the ward sister's office. I stood timidly at the door, as Anne told the sister of our arrival. A tall, friendly person, the sister must have read apprehension writ large, as they say, across my face.

'Well, come in and sit down', she said. I left the heavy suitcase at the door, and perched nervously on the edge of a chair.

'No-one is going to force you to stay here', she said. 'You can go whenever you like. It isn't a prison. You can go home now, if you like . . . but if the specialist thought that you should come in for a while, you'd be wise to stay.'

The sister paused, as she collected together the sheaf of papers necessary for registration. On that miserable Monday morning, I was 'at the end of myself' – I could not even trust my own judgement. Somehow, a still small voice told me that I should stay. Anne was equally certain.

'Now' said the sister. 'Are you going to stay with us for a while?'

'Yes,' I replied.

'Good!' We went through the routine questions – the handful of formalities necessary for admission into mental hospital – and then Anne, who had to return to the accountant's office in which she worked, said good-bye. The taxi driver, hovering in the doorway, seemed relieved that I had agreed to stay.

'After all,' he whispered. 'It ain't such a bad place.'

I suppose he should have known. The hospital was well known in the area. Strange how people reacted to its name, however. Many (ex-patients or their relations) 'swore by it' whilst others seemed to think it was the last

refuge of the true 'nut case'. When I had told one or two
friends that I was going into Cliff Hospital, I was either
congratulated – as if I had secured a place at one of the
best public schools – or pitied. Well, now I would find
out for myself. The swish of the taxi's tyres on the wet
tarmac, and a last hand-wave told me that Anne had
gone.

Sister tidied her papers, and summoned 'Ben'. This
young psychiatric nurse from Bangladesh was the
friendliest and most capable of characters. His face
seemed almost permanently set in a smile.

'This is David,' explained the sister. 'He'll be sharing
a room with Mr Wright. Can you show him where it
is?'

'Of course.' I followed Ben through the house sitting
room and dining hall, through the lobby and up a flight
of carpeted stairs. I was to discover that the house con-
tained about twenty-five patients, and that most shared
rooms. In the men's wing, for example, there were some
six rooms, all pleasantly furnished if a mite small.

'You'll like Mr Wright,' Ben grinned. 'Very nice
man.'

He showed me into a bedroom, and suggested that I
unpack at my leisure. When I replied that at least half
my luggage consisted of books I hoped to read, Ben's
smile grew even wider.

'Oh, well,' he said. 'I hope you get time to read
them.'

He was being his usual diplomatic self. In the month
or so that I stayed in the hospital, I read only one of
those weighty tomes. Ben and I returned downstairs to
the kitchen, where some mid-morning tea had just been
brewed.

'It's very nice here in the summer,' said Ben. I gazed

out of the rain-drenched windows at the tennis-courts outside. The weather seemed far from the 'flaming June' of legend.

'Are you here permanently?' I inquired. He shook his head and explained that a period at Harvey House was just part of his training. Later, he would move on to another part of the hospital, where more serious cases were under treatment.

Harvey House, he explained, was a unit for 'short-term' patients, people who would leave within some three months of admission. Some of the other houses in Cliff Hospital were occupied by far more serious cases, people who required long-term hospitalization. Ben had to depart to complete further work so I was left alone with my thoughts, and my tea and biscuits. I walked over to a chair in the corner of the sitting room, and idly gazed along the bookshelf – a collection of remarkable odds-and-ends including a handsome history of the Church of England. I took Volume 1, and began to glance through it, as I drank my tea. St Aidan! Now, where had I heard that name before? A long time ago, I dreamed that I had arived at a place called 'St Aidan'. I had been so baffled by the dream that I had tried to discover something about St Aidan – now, here he was again in a book in the mental hospital. Where his fellow workers had failed in their task of converting heathen Britain through their preaching, St Aidan had gone forth in the spirit of love and had won men by his example. It was said that when he died, shooting stars were seen in the heavens, as if the very universe saluted a great soul . . .

I left the book and took a brief reconnaissance around the building. No-one seemed interested in me, but then, most of the patients were out on their morning therapy.

What was Anne doing? I wondered. Was it really worth-while, my coming into mental hospital? I stood in the doorway, listening to the rain falling on the trees. There were plenty of trees. The layout of the hospital was simple enough. A number of 'houses' or 'wards' surrounded a large wooded space, which was itself crossed with paths. Thus, if you wanted to obtain some privacy, it was simple enough: you could go for a walk in the woods. Even if an inquisitive grey squirrel crossed your path, you could hardly complain at such intrusion upon your thoughts. I came to know the woods well in the weeks before me. They symbolized that jungle, that tangle, that mixture of flowers and weeds in one's mind. In the end, the hospital could do little more than help you find your own way through to personal reality.

Although I felt aloof on that first dismal morning, I little realized that I was really under observation – not in any 'Big Brother' sense, but to see how I settled down. It was perhaps 'touch and go' whether or not I stayed. It would have been so easy to telephone for a taxi and return home. Not that *that* would have solved any problems. I had been struggling with nervous exhaustion and agoraphobia for a long, long time, perhaps from childhood, when I was evacuated and lived a pillar-to-post existence. For weeks, I had been able to get to work only when accompanied by Anne, since I was terrified of making bus journeys unaided. A kind of invisible barrier seemed to close in upon me, so that the distance I ventured from my home grew less and less almost daily. It was a classic case of that mysterious ailment known as 'agoraphobia', and I had fought with it for years. For example, when I was working in an advertising agency in Nottingham, it was as if an invisible chain permitted me to go only so far from the building. I

can recall going to the open city square, and sadly looking down Wheeler Gate, wanting to go to the bookshop
which was just around the corner, but feeling quite
unable to cross the road. I had sought psychiatric aid
then, as I had when I was in the army, but the results
had been disappointing. The army psychiatrist, a man
in a highly agitated state himself, suggested that all my
problems were due to frustration, sexual and otherwise.
Even though he had recommended that I be excused
various regimental duties, this result did little to help
overcome my problems. To be fair to the army authorities, though, the medical officer at the unit did give me a
week's rest in bed, and gave me strict instructions to take
pheno-barbitone regularly. I reported for the little
white tablets for a time, until I learned that, in the medical officer's opinion, I would have to take them 'for the
rest of my life'. Then only nineteen, I had grave sus-
picions on the taking of drugs, and finally gave up the
treatment.

By an ironic stroke of providence, I was working in
the pharmaceutical industry – and was thus in an excellent position to get advice on drug therapy – when I had
another severe bout of agoraphobia. Of inventive mind,
I managed to find reasons for not attending meetings in
other parts of the country, London, for example. It is
true that I sometimes went to conferences, etc., but I
usually suffered for it – in most of the symptoms that
accompany nervous tension of this type. Sometimes, I
would leave the train or bus miles before my destination
because I suffered such mental agonies. The fact that I
was a church deacon and also studying to be a lay
preacher at this time may seem strange to some: what
hope had I to offer to others? How could I be sure of
reaching my preaching engagements?

I made an appointment to see a psychiatrist in a Midlands town. A man of ample proportions and given to enthusiastic yawns (which displayed a handsome mouthful of fillings) he told me that he also suffered from what he called 'travel sickness'.

'Dear boy,' he said. 'You must take sodium amytal, the best tranquillizer of the lot. I always have some with me.'

I conjured up visions of my chewing drugs like dolly mixtures on some remote railway journey. Certainly, the medicine cabinet at home was full of bottles of drugs, herbal cures and other hopeful attempts to defeat that mental dragon. I felt rather like that man who complained that his moth balls didn't work because throwing them at the moths was such a difficult task. Whatever else was true, I was beginning to learn – way back in the early 1960s – that this mysterious ailment called agoraphobia was remarkably common. A colleague at the office had a similar problem, since his wife could hardly leave the house. On that occasion, a psychiatrist, summoned to the house, had advised the lady to take courage and take up knitting. In the end, my friend had solved the problem by driving his car a few feet from the front door, so that his wife, taking courage in both hands, managed to reach the car, which was then reversed into the garage. As the garage adjoined the house, and a door connected garage and kitchen, the lady was able to get into 'safe surroundings' quickly. The distance between the door and car was increased daily, until my friend's wife achieved what had been thought impossible: she had managed to walk down the garden path to the gate. That 'home remedy' helped cure her agoraphobia, presuming that a permanent cure is possible.

Now I was in a mental hospital, I reflected – was this the end of the road? Encounters with psychiatrists and doctors, and a list of pharmaceutical preparations, rolled through my mind. When, a fortnight previously, I had come to an apparent full stop – I had been almost unable even to move alone in my native city – I had made an appointment with another psychiatrist. I had managed that journey only with the assistance of Anne, and fortunately, I had little time to wait before being summoned to the psychiatrist's office. I had little hopes of the interview. By this time (though I was unaware of the fact) I was suffering from endogenous depression. Thus, I told the psychiatrist, a quietly attentive man, about my problems, and had even typed a brief resume of treatments past and present. I think he must have been a little surprised (even amused) at my 'little list'. But it was for me, a last chance. Had that interview been as fruitless as others gained over the years, I would have returned home, and somehow struggled on.

'God can heal you of all your diseases, physical and mental'. Christians are not slow to remind the anxiety state patient of this truth. I think perhaps they make the mistake of suggesting that Christians are somehow 'excused duties' as I was after I had seen my army psychiatrist. We are all part of the human lot: in the end, we all die. Missionaries have died in foreign fields, just as ministers have 'worn themselves out' here at home: the important miracle is in the transformation of human character, and in that, we may go through many strange experiences, suffering as well as blessing. 'Brother, do you limit God?' No, I do not limit God to take me through any human experience if, in the end, it helps me to help somebody else. So many people have struggled

with the problem of suffering, in a philosophic sense. The person who suffers has to work out his own answers.

The psychiatrist was brief and eminently sensible. He recommended that I take treatment as a hospital patient. I knew, at the back of my mind, that it was the only real answer – but I had not looked forward to making the decision. The psychiatrist summoned Anne from the waiting room, and explained his views to her. Anne nodded in agreement.

'And when would I go in?' I asked timidly.

'Next Monday,' he suggested. In just four days time. It was all arranged so quickly, so smoothly . . .

Indeed, it was something of a small miracle that I had been able to enter hospital so quickly. The psychiatrist was going away on holiday, only the day after I had the appointment, and one or two 'coincidences' had enabled me to see him so quickly.

As a jumble of thoughts scattered through my brain, I stood in the Harvey House doorway and watched the rain. It did not seem to bother the birds very much. The thrushes hopped about, listening for inquisitive worms: perhaps the thrush was the original early bird that caught the worm, I mused. Ben approached.

'You're to see Dr Hunter this afternoon,' he grinned, 'and sister wants to see you for a blood test.'

I followed him to the sister's office.

'Ah, very good,' she smiled. 'Thank you, Ben.'

I sat down as instructed, and sister began to wind the rubber bandage around my arm. I was no stranger to blood tests. A former doctor had considered my pallid expression due to a low haemoglobin count. Sister produced her syringe and carefully made preparations to take a sample of blood. She jabbed the needle into my right arm. Nothing happened. She tried again.

'I think you may have to try my left arm, sister,' I suggested.

'This will be all right,' she said. But still no blood appeared in the syringe.

'You know,' she said with mock anger. 'You've got slippery veins.'

In the end, she had to use the left arm, as I suggested, and the blood sample was finally obtained.

'Slippery veins,' I joked. 'That – and everything else?'

'Hmm,' she said, unwinding the bandage, 'You'll see Dr Hunter after dinner. I wonder what *he'll* make of you . . .!

2

Encounters

As lunch-time approached, the other patients returned from their diverse occupational therapy, for, as sister wisely said, she 'wasn't having patients moping around the building in the morning'. Everyone had to find something to do at the Occupational Therapy Department or at the Arts and Crafts Centre. My room-mate, Mr Wright, proved to be a well-built, bluff and cheerful accountant. To look at him, you would hardly consider this excellent man to be a candidate for a 'nervous breakdown'. In fact, he could remember little of the weekend on which he entered Cliff Hospital. This was, he explained, the second breakdown; the first had been less serious, but his employers had ignored the warning signs which he himself recognized. Thus, his requests for assistance in his department had been ignored, lost or delayed (it is never easy to tell which in a large organization) until he had finally collapsed. I liked Mr Wright at once. He was a jovial man in his late forties, and lived only a few miles from the hospital. His employers were concerned about his progress, and sent him reports on the department in which he had been previously engaged – a mixed blessing, one might say, for one suffering with the effects of overwork. It seemed as if his employers regarded his stay in a mental hospital as a desirable emotional retraining ready for greater business battles ahead. If this seems strange, the author may add that he has observed similar behaviour in other companies where men, instead of being driven to mental illness, have taken to alcohol or (in wiser cases) quit.

Mr Wright was accompanied by Bruce, a very serious-minded young chemist, who had been preparing to sit his final degree examinations when he suffered his breakdown. Both men had been at Cliff for a few weeks, and both expressed a sense of great improvement since admission.

'I couldn't even face reading a paper when I came in here,' said Bruce. 'Nothing in print made any sense to me at all . . . it was just a jumble.'

I recognized the symptoms, for I had suffered similar sensations myself only a few weeks earlier.

The heated meal trolley arrived from the kitchen just a few houses away, and lunch was served by a couple of the nurses. There was always plenty of food to go around. Ken and Bruce joined me at a table, and we tucked in accordingly. My appetite was better than I had anticipated. At home, when I was alone in the house, I tended to live on a plate of soup or cereals, until Anne came home in the evening and prepared a cooked meal. I was now able to observe some of the other patients – there were about twenty present at the meal (a few were away on extended leave) and most were about my own age, that is between 35 and 50. About a quarter of the patients were younger, however. Lucille, an attractive brunette in her late teens, for example, was sitting at a table with three ladies, all old enough to be her mother. The atmosphere was more one of a good private hotel than a hospital, I reflected – and, at that point, sister appeared with the 'drugs wagon'. This was a trolley – the size, approximately, of a large pram – in which various pharmaceutical preparations were kept, neatly labelled in bottles. Every patient was prescribed a course of medication by one of the staff psychiatrists, and sister handed out the appropriate tablets to patients after each meal. She made sure that the tablets were taken. To one patient, who promised to take the drugs 'later on', sister replied sternly.

'It's part of my job to *see* you take them.' End of argument. I was not given any tablets for, as sister reminded me, I had to see Dr Hunter first. As far as I could tell, most patients were taking some form of anti-depressant as well as other tablets, e.g. tranquillizers, sedatives, etc. Most laymen (like the television advertisements) use the word 'depression' to mean a sort of 'browned-off' feeling. In medicine, however, depression is a real illness, affecting – or creating changes in – the biochemistry of the brain. The amphetamines, which have caused so many problems on the illegal drug scene, were originally developed for anti-depression therapy in hospitals, and later used in general practice. Their addictive properties caused too many problems, however, and a new range of anti-depression drugs are used in hospitals now. As I was to find, the dosage prescribed by the psychiatrist is usually the minimum compatible with effective treatment – but, watching sister hand out the pills was something of an education. One middle-aged lady had no less than five different drugs to take after each meal, though one must add that hers was a somewhat rare condition.

After lunch, we adjourned to the sitting room and tea was served. Some of the patients relaxed, closing their eyes to get a cat-nap, others talked. We had to stay there, because the hospital staff (including the psychiatrist that I was to see) did their weekly rounds on Monday afternoons at two o'clock precisely.

I sat next to Ken Wright and asked him what I was required to do when the doctors' round commenced.

'Well,' he said with mock seriousness. 'They all come in and ask us, one by one, how we are. We all say, "Very well, thank you", and, when that's all over, we all leave and they stay here to discuss our cases.'

He returned to sipping his tea.

'What shall I say when they come to me?' I asked.

'Just tell 'em you're a new boy,' my friend responded.

'But what good does all that do?' I persisted.

'Well, it's just courtesy, and they're supposed to be able to tell how you are, by looking at you.' Hmmm, I felt slightly green, and was still wondering about a possible taxi ride home. However, the doctors arrived, and with sister, went around the sitting room, and inquired of each of us, how we were feeling today. Bruce said something about not being able to sleep, and sister made a note.

'Thank you very much', sister and when the round was finished. 'We would like this room for a conference now, but please don't go faraway, because the doctors will be wanting to see some of you individually.' As it happened, I was one of the first called in. I walked down the corridor with little enough confidence. Which of the psychiatrists was Dr Hunter? I tapped at the open door.

'Hello . . . you're Mr Lazell. Good, sit down, will you?'

Dr Hunter was a young man, perhaps thirty, smartly but quietly dressed and with a gentle manner. He pulled from his file a recent copy of 'The Christian Record' in which I had written of my mental illness.

'You wrote this, didn't you?'

'I rushed it off when I knew I might have to come into hospital.'

He smiled. Perhaps it was the first time that the arrival of a patient had been announced in the pages of a religious weekly. It was Dr Hunter's quiet, competent approach that changed my attitude to the mental hospital. This was to be the first of several talks between the young doctor and myself, and, these weeks later, I hardly recall what was said in that initial discussion. I recall only amazement that here was a psychiatrist who was 'on my wavelength'. After that interview, I felt that I had a golden opportunity to obtain some real understanding of my mental illness. All thoughts of returning home were gone now. I felt that I wanted to co-operate fully with the hospital treatment – and, as I was a life-long rebel against authority, this was no mean victory for the authorities, had they but known it!

My new friend, Ken Wright, noticed my more buoyant attitude when I returned to the dining room.

'Decided to stay, have you?' he grinned.

'Just as long as the food lasts', I replied.

'Oh, well, you're all right then', he said. 'They'll never run out of porridge and semolina pudding in this place.'

As it had stopped raining, I took a short stroll along the road, and found myself at the hospital shop, which was closed (though only for a short while, as the good lady in charge had gone for the inevitable cup of tea). The hospital chapel was nearby, and I looked at the list of services. As I did, the door opened, and the chaplain – a genial man in a darned cassock – came out.

'Hello', he said – as if he and I were respectively Livingstone and Stanley meeting in some distant place after much anticipation. 'How are you?' (It was always hard to know how to answer people's inquiries because one never knew exactly who they were! One day I discovered that the 'staff electrician' with whom I had lengthily discussed wiring problems, was actually a fellow patient!

'I'm not sure if I should talk to you,' I replied. The chaplain looked puzzled.

'I'm a Methodist', I added, 'and I think you Anglicans have just decided you wouldn't have us.'

'Ah, well that wasn't *my* fault,' he replied, and, adding a further welcome to any of the Wednesday night services, he departed. I cannot say that, in any denominational sense, the church was very strong at the hospital. The only time that I went to a Wednesday night evensong, I noticed that about ten people were present. Yet practical Christianity was evident everywhere – and this was to be one of the most important lessons that emerged from my weeks in hospital.

That first day at Harvey House came to its close . . . In the evening, I gazed at the television set in the sitting room, had a welcome cup of hot chocolate at nine o'clock, and decided to have 'an early night'.

The night sister, attired in a smart green uniform came on duty at about half-past eight, when the doors of the building were locked, that is, the doors leading to the hospital grounds.

'That to keep us in?' I asked one of the nurses wryly.

'Certainly not,' she replied. 'It's to keep everyone else out.'

The night sister was invariably a kindly, perhaps plump person, whose task was to be the guardian angel of the house. She distributed the 'last thing at night' medication – like sleeping tablets – and was responsible for looking after us until the morning. On the two or three occasions that I wandered downstairs at about two a.m. (perhaps because I could not sleep or had indigestion) I found the night sister alert, if somewhat surprised by the sudden appearance of the new and rather unpredictable patient. Nerves play many strange tricks, however. One night, soaked with perspiration, I wandered downstairs and asked the night sister to take my temperature, certain that it was least 104°. The task was performed and the night sister gazed at the thermometer thoughtfully.

'96.6°,' she said. 'That's quite below normal. Nothing to worry about.'

'Funny that,' I replied. 'Sister told me I've got slippery veins.'

'Ah, well,' smiled the night sister. 'Maybe you're a slippery customer.'

3

Therapy

Although I want to make a summary of conclusions in a later chapter, it is perhaps useful to pause and look at phobias – agoraphobia, in particular. In recent years, this strange malady has become so common that it is written up in many popular magazines. Not that a cure seems any nearer. Rather like a dense cloud that covers the sun, one has to wait for the shadow to depart. Therapy, in or out of hospital, helps move the cloud along, sometimes even disperses it, but, since those un-natural fears that we call 'phobias' are so deeply buried in the mind, it is perhaps doubtful that the patient ever makes a *full* recovery. However, the improvement in the life-style of the patient can be so impressive that treat-ment is always worth the attempt.

In former times, it was fashionable to talk of 'a nervous breakdown'. Medically, there is no such ailment; doctors now speak of 'anixety states' or 'debility'. It reminds one of the man lost for words when attempting to describe an elephant to a man who had never seen one: 'I cannot describe it, but I'll know one when I see it'. If sufficient pressures are exerted upon the indi-vidual, he will crack up at some point, developing an ailment that doctors may call 'psychosomatic', that is, physical manifestations springing from a state of mind, or spirit. I met one or two patients in the mental hos-pital, who were equally candidates for a coronary thrombosis. Fortunately for them, their 'breakdown threshold' was lower than that of a man who literally drives himself to death through over-activity, or attempting to manage too many situations. In these days, when so much in medicine seems to be linked to the state of mind, or spirit, of the patient, we might well examine the local church as a therapy centre. Do we feel, after the service, that it was *good for us* to be there? Or was it just another meeting?

In many cases a breakdown goes hand in hand with over-work, that is, trying to manage too many situations. It is difficult to be dogmatic here as I'm told that often the overwork is a symptom of the breakdown rather than the cause, for over-anxious people can drive themselves to overwork. Nevertheless if it is true that hard work never killed anyone it is equally certain that trying to handle too many jobs can cause a breakdown. This is one reason why so many social workers, ministers and active laymen in our churches are suffering breakdowns. For the most part, we do not share the work equally in our churches, so that the newcomer feels that he is really unable to contribute any of his talents, whilst the members of the overworked church management committee have long since lost the joy of their work – it has become just a succession of problems to discuss.

One of the most important lessons one gains through illness is the realization of this truth: that when Jesus said, 'Without me, you can do nothing', he was stating no less than the truth, just as resting in the Lord is, in its proper time, every bit as vital as going out to evangelize. Like many people in the church today, I had taken on too many jobs, and gained little satisfaction from any of them. The Christian writer has special problems, anyway, and as I was helping prepare a book manuscript for an evangelist I had plenty of work to handle in my 'spare time'.

In addition, the mail connected with the work I was handling for the Beam Fellowship for Christian Communication was often quite considerable, so that I spent most of my Sundays at the typewriter. I don't know if the advice given on church magazines, local radio and sundry other matters proved useful (Christians are notoriously slow at answering letters) but I had little time left for relaxation. In addition, I had somehow become identified locally as 'a Christian with a ready ear', so that people feeling 'depressed' sometimes came to see me. On the Friday before I went into mental hospital, I received a phone call.

'Mr. So-and-so is coming down to have a chat with you. He is feeling so depressed, and I'm sure you can help him . . .'

I had abandoned my appointments as a local preacher, but I might as well have been in a pulpit as pounding the typewriter. In any case, though I felt a great desire to help those who wrote or visited me, I began to feel 'flat' . . . I gained little satisfaction from going to church, rarely read my Bible, and felt that there was little in life that really interested me. However, I was still very interested in old books about 'the old time preachers' and it was this interest that sustained my faith in those dismal months. That, and my family. Our two children, Michael (13) and Kerry (11) had developed into active, intelligent youngsters, overshadowing Anne and I in size!

Alas, I failed to take sufficient interest in my family. I do not mean that I was deliberately ignorant of their activities. Michael, being a far better Scout than I was at his age, can show his dad more than a few things! Rather, it was as if I had somehow come to burn the

spiritual candle at both ends. In the end, I became 'a
burned out Christian'. You are fortunate indeed if such
people do not exist in your church. Thus, when I arrived at mental hospital, I was not expecting a spiritual
experience, in the sense of feeling, at the end of my stay,
'truly the Lord was here'. But the way for my arrival
had been paved, nevertheless. Take, for example, the
matter of therapy. As I have explained, every patient
had to find some suitable task for morning occupation.
On my third morning at the hospital, a bright sunny
day, I was instructed to go down to the Occupational
Therapy Unit. My heart sank. In school, making raffia
mats, or chisel racks in woodwork had proved such dis-
asters that I was accused of having 'two pairs of feet and
no hands at all'. My art teacher, normally a man of
patience, regarded me as a one-man disaster area when
it came to 'using my hands'. That influence has remained; even when gardening – which is rare enough –
I manage to pull up the seedlings that my wife has just
planted, leaving the weeds to flourish undisturbed.
Thus, my journey to the Occupational Therapy Unit
was not exactly filled with high hopes.

It was a lovely morning, and the flowers looked
brighter than ever. A squirrel clambered down a tree so
that he could take a good look at me. He paused with his
front paws in the air, his body assuming a sort of question mark. Then he turned, and ran into the under-
growth, amazed, no doubt, at the kind of patient going
down to Occupational Therapy these days. I walked
slowly, consoling myself that, if the worst came to the
worst, I could always telephone for that taxi home. Finally, I arrived at the long, low red building which was
my destination. Drawing a deep breath, I pushed
through the swing doors and went inside. It was a cheer-

ful enough place, with groups of patients working on various projects – like the making of large, cuddly teddy bears, ornamental trays, wickerwork baskets, and so on. Most of the patients were women, many – no doubt – long-term patients. The words of my old art teacher lingered in my mind. Any teddy bear that I attempted to make would probably turn out to be an oddly-stuffed sealion. It was with little enough confidence that I discussed my errand with a member of the staff, a tall bespectacled man in an immaculate white coat.

'You'd be surprised at the high standard of work we turn out here' he said, 'and patients are allowed to take home the objects they make. They just pay for the materials.'

My heart sank further. My son, Michael, is very good at woodwork, and, even though a polite enough lad, he would obviously pass some comment at the lop-sided and quite unusable tray that I would surely construct. I decided to continue my search for something to do, elsewhere.

'I'll go away and think about it,' I told the instructor. One or two of the patients smiled at me, as I left. My next stop was the Arts Department. I had heard rumours of a small printing unit somewhere in the hospital, and, as I was once a compositor and printer, considered that a job there would be something I could manage. I was nevertheless surprised to find that the 'Press Room' (as the printing unit was called) was part of the Arts Department, itself managed by one of the most hard-working, patient ladies that I have ever met – Mrs Dundry. By another of those odd 'coincidences', the young man who had been helping in the Press Room had been discharged the previous Friday, so Mrs Dundry was pleasantly surprised when I appeared and offered to do some type-setting.

'We can certainly do with some help' she explained. Originally, the large Adana printing machine had been introduced as an optional extra in therapy, but the machine had proved so useful – in the thousand and one print jobs that every hospital needs – that incoming work had mounted. I agreed to start 'work' the following day, and felt quite pleased that I could set some type again after all those years. And it was indeed surprising how quickly I picked up the routine again . . .

The sister smiled when I told her that I had decided to work in the Arts Department.

'I would have sent you there in the first place,' she said. 'But you told me that you had no interest in that direction.'

Yes, it was true. But the Arts Department was a refreshing contrast to my school art classes where the height of originality was that of drawing two saucepans instead of one, from the model saucepan on display. Mrs Dundry was amazingly patient and encouraging with those in her charge. They could draw, or paint, whatever they chose. Some of the work was excellent, and the department produced posters for the various social events taking place in the hospital – the annual fete, for example, or the dances held at the social centre. My good friend, Ken Wright, spent his mornings in the Art Department, where he exuded a spirit of good cheer, as he produced a variety of water-colours. Some of them were so well done that I suggested he submit them to one of the banks as possible pictorial cheque designs. I spent my mornings setting type for medicine bottle labels and other hospital requirements, sometimes printing them on the large Adana. The room was sun-lit, and I enjoyed the work, so that the time passed quickly. On one or two occasions, the telephone rang to tell Mrs Dundry that Ken and I were wanted 'immediately' for a group therapy meeting. It was always a little frustrating to leave a printing job half-finished, but then, I was first a *patient*, then a printer. The group therapy meetings, held two or three times a week, were those in which the patients' psychiatrist would lead a group in the discussion of our problems. One day, when Ken and I had rushed back from the Arts Department, we were greeted with the message 'as doctor has been delayed, will you start the meeting among yourselves, please. Doctor suggests that David Lazell can start things off'. In one sense I did, as I carried most of the chairs into the sunny pavilion in which our group met. By the time that all the patients in our group had arrived (there were about eight of us) Ken and I had started our discussion. After talking first about the purpose of the group, we spent the time drawing up questions that we would like to ask our psychiatrist. For example, we were interested in knowing whether the number of broken marriages that he saw, put him off getting married himself. And so, on that memorable morning, the psychiatrist arrived to find himself at the receiving end of our questions. I think he must have regarded me with just a little suspicion after that, but the meeting was one of the most interesting we had attended. In seeing some of our problems from the psychiatrist's point of view, we were helped to put our own problems into perspective. One of the most moving moments in any of our group meetings was that when Irene – a short lady of about fifty – told us of her work in the long-term 'sick' patients ward. Irene was not given to conversation. In fact, she usually remained silent during our therapy meetings. However, I asked her to tell us something about her work in the sick wards, and, for ten minutes or so, she told us of the problems faced in helping disorientated older patients.

'It's such hard work that sometimes I think that I'll not go today . . . and then I remember their smiles when they see me come into their ward. At the end of every day I'm there, they say, "You will come back again, won't you?".'

In another meeting, Tim told us about his difficulties in obtaining employment. A smart, middle-aged man with considerable experience in the transport industry, Tim could be discharged from the hospital as soon as he found a job. But the job was proving elusive.

'As soon as you say you're from Cliff Hospital, they don't want to know you,' he said. I tried to point out that the job-seeker often encountered prejudice on the part of the interviewer. On at least one occasion, I was rejected because I had mentioned (in the hobbies and part-time interests in the application form) that I helped in a church youth club. It seemed that some companies did not want Christians; others did not want former patients of Cliff.

'I suppose it's best to be dishonest . . . not to tell them that you've been in here'. Tim was understandably bitter about the disappointment he had suffered. The shadow of a breakdown can stay with a person: I wondered how Bruce would survive in the outside world. A young man of considerable sensitivity, he would be especially vulnerable to comments about his stay in hospital. On the other hand, Wilson – who had worked in advertising – managed to find a job with comparatively little difficulty. He had been appointed publicity manager for a small but go-ahead engineering company. For a few days, he went to work from the hospital, returning to the house at night. Later, he was discharged, and now is leading a useful life in the community. Before he left, I asked him how he was getting along with his new job.

'Okay!' he said. 'But you know what advertising is . . . I'm sorting out all the muddles left by the last chap.'

We swopped a few tales of our experiences in the advertising business, in which breakdowns are not infrequent. It is true that some jobs seem to have a relatively high breakdown factor. Strangely enough, one of these seems to be nursing itself. We asked the group psychiatrist if he thought there were emotional dangers peculiar to his calling, and he said – wisely – that any job demanding personal involvement possessed these danger factors. Recalling ministers and local preachers who had suffered emotional problems, I saw his point. Yet, although our psychiatrist clearly had sympathies with the Christian faith (and was probably a Christian himself) we rarely brought up the matter of personal faith during our discussions. Perhaps this is because the local church has become known for its too-occasional witness, in the sense that someone needing help would, more often than not, find the church either closed or unready (not unwilling, but unprepared) for effective counselling. The hospice of former ages performed the function of 'open house' in the community, but we have little like it today. Thus, people with personal hang-ups often turn to drinks or drugs for some kind of answer. Some try to live with their problems, so that *evident* mental illness is probably the tip of the iceberg. In the weeks immediately prior to my going into hospital, this fact became increasingly evident, in my own contacts at least. When I swopped advertising experiences with the cheerful Wilson, I might have mentioned one of my saddest experiences. That had to do with a secretary in the agency in which I was once employed. Rosemary was a fine, well-educated girl, who was engaged to a young business executive. To all appearances, he was doing well, and had the prospect of promotion. One may not know the pressures that were concealed, but one day, he attempted to kill himself. This attempt failed, and hospital treatment saved him. Rosemary suffered a tremendous shock, as the reader will well understand, but agreed to go ahead with the wedding when her fiance recovered. She spent a lot of time with him, and finally went to his parents' home for a short holiday. It was there that, without any kind of warning, he made a second attempt at suicide – and on this occasion succeeded. One could not but wonder why he had been untouched by hope for the future. Rosemary was a Christian; the wedding was to have taken place in church. Presumably, the young man had been counselled by social workers before he left hospital after his first suicide attempt. Depression is often concealed by the cheerful face; we too often assume that our friends, family, congregations are secure in their faith. Churches on both sides of the Atlantic may yet be called to a far greater work in the area of spiritual therapy than they have yet imagined. I discussed this matter with the psychiatrist one day in a personal session.

'I wonder why I go to church,' I told him. 'It so often seems irrelevant to my situation. It is so easy to feel quite alone in the church congregation'. He agreed.

'Maybe you have this kind of insight for a purpose,' he suggested. 'Maybe you can help others who feel the same way that you do'.

Even in our group discussions, the psychiatrist 'threw the ball back into our court', for the purpose of the hospital was basically that of helping us, as individuals, to discover the right answer to our own problems. In that sense, the mental hospital is both a retreat and a re-training centre. Even with the benefits of modern treatment and drugs, there is no final answer: healing is a process that springs from within. As Jesus promised to the woman at the well, life has to be a spring welling up from within. It is interesting to note that many patients talk of their pre-hospital days as being 'dry', as if some inner spiritual thirst was not being satisfied. Wilson told us of a group called People Not Psychiatrists, and of his involvement in it. Quite simply, this was a group which met in a home, sharing their experiences and enjoying a fellowship. Whilst not anti-psychiatrist, the members of the group realized that they could be liberated in relationships – in love, one for another. Many such groups exist in Britain today, under diverse titles. In some ways, they represent the essence of true religion – in finding oneself. Jesus saw people as they were intended to be. It is interesting to note that he rarely judged other people, and saved his wrath for the so-called religious people who had strangled the sense of God's love. I wonder how he might react to much of our church life today.

Our group therapy had plenty of laughs – sometimes, we made jokes at the psychiatrist's expense, and he took them in good spirit. Although some people said, before the session, that they thought the meetings a waste of time, it was interesting to see how they became involved. Maybe the same is true of potential groups within the local church. 'Bear ye, one another's burdens' the scriptures tell us. In the final analysis, that was precisely what we attempted to do. If we did not say much about God, the discussions led to the heart of faith, because they were about people trying to find meaning in a frantic world.

4

The Community

One day, the sister defined her task as that of shaping a therapeutic community, in which members would help one another as far as they could. Living in a community always has its problems, simply because people react to hospital environment – and its inevitable rules and regulations – in different ways. One of our number, for example, a man whose marriage seemed to be 'on the rocks' almost went out of his way to break hospital rules, like smoking in areas where smoking was forbidden. I found much to like in Barry, but he was certainly unpredictable, given to quite violent changes of mood. He seemed to care little about his wife or two young daughters, and wandered off into the woods (in which it was easy to conceal oneself) when they were due to arrive for a visit. Then, just as his wife was about to depart, he would reappear, full of apologies. I could never discover the root of this irrational behaviour, this strange love-hate relationship towards his family. Perhaps the psychiatrists were more successful, but I doubt it. In the end, Barry just left the hospital, as erratic as ever – though, I hasten to add, quite capable of looking after himself. He was not the only one who, somehow failed to gain anything from the care of the hospital staff. One or two others discharged themselves, perhaps in moments of discouragement, because, as they said, 'I don't think I am getting anywhere.'

Recovering from a breakdown can be a long and painful process (for example, I recently heard of a Christian, a former nurse, who has been a patient in a mental hospital for four years). This is true of other illnesses, too, but people can be less sympathetic towards those who *appear* to have nothing wrong with them. Flora Klickmann, the former editor of 'The Girls Own Paper', wrote an excellent record of her own breakdown in a best-seller ('The Flower Patch Among the Hills') and in a subsequent book on mental illness said that she thought it a pity that people with genuine 'nerve problems' did not break out in a rash of purple spots, so that it became an evident, accepted illness. One may meet, in a mental hospital, people who have been former patients, but who decided to leave before they had really recovered – and then, in a subsequent time of strain, had fallen ill, worse than before. Thus, in our house, we did share much of each other's problems. We tried to encourage one another in our conversations.

In a very real sense, the victory of someone like Wilson was a victory for all of us. One of the saddest cases was that of Kathleen, a young woman from the North of England. Before moving to our part of the world, she had seen a specialist for her anxiety state, and, for some obscure reason, had been placed on a massive dosage of a well-known tranquillizer. Her condition deteriorated, and following a move of home, she consulted the head psychiatrist at our hospital – a man of considerable perception. At once, he saw that she was in need of hospital treatment, and Kathleen had been inside some weeks before I arrived. Even then, she found it difficult to cross the room unaided because, as she explained, 'the floor seemed to rock about like a boat'. Sister explained that, however unpleasant the situation was, Kathleen would have to persevere with unaided walking if she was to get well. Nevertheless, Kathleen sometimes came up to me and whispered,

'Do you mind if I hold your arm when you cross the room? I don't think I can make it on my own!' Her husband, a fine man, drove a great distance to visit the hospital, sometimes taking Kathleen for short walks, though more often, she preferred to sit in the car. He was obviously devoted to his wife, and although Kathleen faced a tough time in overcoming her anxiety state and the effects of large dosages of drugs (that is before she had come to the hospital) I felt that she had a good future. That was one of the lessons I learned; it was important to see the best in people, to encourage their sometimes faltering steps towards normal life in the world beyond the gates. There is, indeed, a message for the evangelist and pastor in that, for our spiritual walk is often as feeble and as uncertain as the steps that Kathleen took across the room.

Ken Wright and I did our good deed for the community two or three times daily, as we wheeled the heated meals trolley to a ward kitchen further up the road. We had to collect the meals for our house, and always tried to make the trip in record time. Indeed, we became so adept at wheeling the trolley, spilling the gravy into the custard on only one occasion, that we wondered if we might challenge one or two of the other wards in a kind of 'hospital trolley Monte Carlo' event. The contest never materialized, however, which is probably just as well! The ward sister (or charge nurse – the gentleman who relieved the sister) thought Ken and I so good at handling the meals trolley that they rarely asked anyone else to make the errand. It was always 'Ken and David – time to collect the meal'. And, with cries of encouragement from the others, we set off. It was of course, a little joke in the community, and one day, Mr Dickens, the charge nurse, announced very gravely that the hospital authorities were considering putting me on the permanent staff as Meals Trolley Manager. The trolley was quite massive – after all, it had to convey meals for twenty or thirty people – and had unpredictable wheels. Sometimes, they braked themselves, in which even Ken and I had to do some on-the-spot adjustments. After one especially tricky piece of manoeuvering with the trolley one day, Ken said thoughtfully, 'I wonder if you can take exams in this sort of thing.'

'Sure thing,' I replied. 'But you'd have to go to the Massachusetts Institute of Technology.'

'Victoria and Albert Museum, you mean,' chuckled Ken.

Other minor chores were allocated to all of us, the intention being that of keeping the house spick and span. It was almost like being back in the army again, when one studied 'Orders' to check with duties one had to perform. Hospital life, I am glad to report, was far less strenuous than national service, and my chore was usually that of sweeping the stairs. I usually started from the top and worked my way down, in time to meet Ken who was sweeping the entrance and lining up the mats. Presenting broom in best military style, I congratulated Ken on a job well done. These chores had to be completed before one went off for occupational therapy in the morning, so there was a great coming-and-going after breakfast. Ken and I then waited for the lady who brought the newspapers – as well as detergents, sweets, chocolates, cigarettes and other useful items – at about 8.45 a.m. As we were the last ward to be visited, the selection of newspapers was rather limited – sometimes to a single copy of 'The Sun'. One morning, I ambled over to the car with a dollar bill in my hand, and inquired of the lady (in an exaggerated American accent), 'Say, do you ever get "The Christian Science Monitor"?' Ken chuckled, as the lady looked dumbfounded. She probably thought I was one of the more serious cases from another ward.

'Well,' the newspaper lady replied. 'We'll be glad to bring out any paper that you want to order every day. On the other hand, you don't look as though you'll be here for very long.'

In what sense that was meant, I could merely guess.

Rumour had it that the brightest stars in the hospital firmament shone in our house, and we did have visitors from other wards. Most of these were young people who ambled in, late in the evening, quite near locking-up time. The conversation between sister and one of the intruders – Sally, for example, the plump and often aimless twenty-year-old from the next house – was always worth hearing.

'Hello, Sally. You can't stay long. We're locking up.'

'I only want to stay a minute to talk to . . .'

Sally, lighting a cigarette, would fade into a paroxysm of coughing.

'And those don't do you any good, either.'

'Well, you've got to die sometime haven't you?' Sally beamed and blinked at the rest of the patients, who had been trying to listen to the television programme.

'Have you told your own charge nurse that you're down here?'

'Mr Hughes? He doesn't worry about *me*. He lets me do what I like.'

A mild exaggeration, to say the least.

'Well, I can give you five minutes, Sally . . . then I'm locking up.'

Sister would turn to go to her office. Then Sally would pipe up, 'How do you get a transfer to this ward?'

'You don't. Everyone is allocated to the unit that suits them best.'

'Well, how did they know that Humphries Ward suited me best. No-one asked me.'

There would follow a discussion – lasting well beyond the five minutes promised by the sister – on the reasons why various patients were placed in specific wards. Sally, a happy enough person, seemed to possess the knack of reducing any reasoned discussion to a shambles.

Then, one of the older ladies would snap, 'I wish you'd go home, Sally. I was listening to the television before you came in.'

'Television . . . fat lot of good that does anyone . . .'

Then, as if the previous ten minutes had been entirely placid, Sally would stand and announce that she was going to bed.

'Goodnight, everyone.' Sally ambled out, closely followed by one of the nurses, delegated to lock up.

I once discussed Sally's case with a member of the staff – not in any depth, of course, because treatment is always confidential. But Sally was in that peculiar category of the 'the permanent patient'. She was, in fact, 'hospitalized' to the extent that she could not face life in the outside world. At weekends, she went home to see her parents who lived nearby, and, from what she told me, her room was well decorated and furnished. However, she had no desire to return home on a permanent basis; her home was the hospital.

'Sally is such a useful person,' one of the staff told me. 'We've made a lot of use of her, and haven't realized that all the time we were making her more dependent on hospital routine. We have tried to get her out, but she just does not have the will or the strength spiritually, to face the outside world.'

This was perhaps a tribute to the success of the therapeutic community concept. In times of religious revival, people find it hard to leave the church in which they worship – but, most of our lives, we shoot out the moment the service is over. We do not depend on our church life, nor even – in practice – upon the Gospel. In talking with people like Sally, I felt that some practical expression of the Christian faith offered the only real answer. Doesn't belief in our selves, our integrity and our possibilities rest upon a religious view of life? I didn't say much about Christian ideals at the hospital, but, on more than one occasion, tried to lift Sally's vision just a little.

'You know, you are such a useful sort of person – a good worker, when you put your mind to it. Your parents would like to have you home, and you could certainly get a good job.'

Sally, puffing on the inevitable cigarette, made some kind of excuse. I still wonder what will happen to her. One day, she will have to be discharged . . . and what then? It was as if she had opted out of making any decisions.

As a patient, I did not think myself competent to give anyone any advice – but I learned (at least a little) to listen to other people. For example, I would be setting up some type in the Press Room when one of the older, long-term patients came in to talk to me.

'My wife left me. I still don't know why. Would you know why she left me?'

I attempted to steer the conversation round to the view from the window, where some beautiful flower beds were close at hand. I might be in the middle of a conversation of this kind, when I would turn to find that the patient had gone. Some were unable to converse in any depth; one dear man's sole method of communication to others was a smile and a military salute.

'Don't mind him,' Ken Wright told me. 'He's one of the regulars. We call him the Field Marshal.'

I wondered what the world looked like to that apparently happy man. Did he touch reality at any point? Was his salute the only gesture he recalled from a happier youth?

And so we always smiled and saluted in return. It was, at that moment, the only way we knew to touch him – to convey our fellow-humanity. In its own way, it was a sort of sermon in which we recalled our common need of help beyond ourselves.

5

A Walk Through the Woods

The telephone kiosk was not such a temptation as it first appeared, for when I went to use it, I discovered it was out of order. There was another kiosk somewhere in the hospital grounds, so I asked one of the nurses where it might be found. She pointed to a path that ran through the woods.

'Go down there,' she smiled. 'You can't miss it.'

Her view of my local geography was highly optimistic, for the kiosk proved elusive enough. There were several paths that one could take, and I must have taken the wrong turning (no doubt watched by inquisitive sparrows and hopping thrushes) at least twice, for I found myself at the lawn fringing the 'Mother and Child Unit'. This was an attractive setting, with groups of women and children sitting on the lawn, shaded from the sun by bright red parasols. Many women suffer some form of temporary mental disturbance at pregnancy – indeed, a Christian worker of my own acquaintance had some months of treatment at this very unit. Following the termination of her pregnancy (or, to put it better, the birth of her baby son) Chrissie seemed to lose all sense of time, space and even identity. The boundaries of mental and physical illness cannot be fixed, though some Christians sometimes make 'snap judgements' which skilled specialists would hesitate to underline. Chrissie, for example was ill for some three months, but made a full recovery, in which the interest and prayers of her friends at her church played a good part. However, I did not consider myself a candidate for similar treatment, so I re-traced my footsteps through the wood. It was a very pleasant setting . . . one could come out here and be quite alone (and that, I think, is sometimes very important for the anxiety state patient). Sometimes, I went for a walk with one or two of the others, and we would make up jokes as we went along. Sometimes, I tried to use the opportunity to encourage one or other of the patients. Lucille, for example, was always good company, even though I felt that she had little confidence in her own future. She was a fine girl, just twenty or so, attractive and with real ability. But she suffered from depression. I always had high hopes of Lucille, for I recognized in her, some of the battles I had faced (and sometimes lost) in earlier life. It is said that everyone has to find his or her own truth through experience, and this is so often true in mental illness. We so rarely realize that others that we meet every day, or with whom we worship every Sunday, have much the same problems. A gospel song says, 'If we could see beyond today . . .' In the woods, along the picturesque paths, one could lose a sense of time, and meditate. One's problems seemed less important. I even forgot that I was really searching for the telephone kiosk – the one that worked! – that night I returned to Harvey to discover a new arrival.

Andy was possessed of a permanent beam on his face. He seemed just about the very last candidate for a mental hospital, and as he was an out-and-out Christian, witnessing to staff and patients alike, one had to look hard for any signs of mental imbalance. In the end, I forgot what little psychology I learned at college and asked him why he was at the hospital. He explained that he had been working very hard (probably far too hard – that was so often the case with younger patients) building up his own business. He had been unwell, and started to develop odd symptoms. One of these was the belief that he controlled the speech of other people.

'It is as if I literally put the words into other people's mouths,' he said. 'The whole world started to get a bit strange after that, so I went along to the doctor – and was soon in here.'

Andy was popular enough. When one day, I suggested a walk in the woods, we found ourselves followed by about half-a-dozen others. I pointed out important landmarks, like the tree 'up which the psychiatrist does his best thinking'. Andy was always good for a joke, and invariably managed to top any mild jest I made. At home, was Andy the same? Or was this a cover for a more serious mental illness? I believe that Andy was fundamentally himself. As leader of a Christian youth fellowship, he was never short of visitors. One night, I met a charming – if rather quaintly dressed – girl of about seventeen, and as she was talking to Andy, joined the conversation.

'I expect you're missing Andy back at the church?'

'A bit,' the young lady agreed. 'You see, he keeps us in order.'

Andy blushed.

'Well, someone's got to do it,' he said.

When I asked him about the activities of his youth group, he mentioned a list as long as his arm. Many of the activities he mentioned were of a basic spiritual, rather than a social nature – giving out tracts, for example.

Some might ask, 'Well, if he was doing such important work, why did the good Lord send Andy into a mental hospital?' I think the answers could be many. Certainly, Andy was unwell – despite his buoyant and bronzed appearance – and he needed help. Like many others involved in youth work, he was trying to do too much, and, remembering that he was running his own business, too (and was also married), one can see how pressures built up. You could compare it to doing without sleep. Although I have been to all-night prayer meetings, I do not find it my given ministry. Indeed, I am usually exhausted by ten o'clock at night, and am often in bed even before that. Christians who, for some reason, had to do without sleep for a long period would suffer from disorientation, mental distress, etc. Similar symptoms can arise through overtaxing the mind in other ways. There is nothing sinful about having a nervous breakdown; neither has it to do with loss of faith. Andy, as a youth worker, would probably have to counsel young people in trouble during later life, and there is little doubt that a stay in mental hospital would give him considerable insight into handling people with problems. In addition, he was certainly a ready advertisement for his faith. Because mental hospitals are made to house people with depression and other mental ailments, it is important that someone present should possess the 'gift' or 'therapy' of laughter. Andy was so radiant a character that he was able to cheer up those who might otherwise have thought of their own problems. He was not an escapist. He knew that entry into mental hospital was a serious step, especially as this meant being away from his business. But he had sufficient faith to believe that the Lord had left him no option.

We were, of course, very fortunate to be in so pleasant a setting. During the preparation of this small book, I have received letters from other Christians suffering from mental illness (in and out of hospital) and have been deeply moved by reports of poor conditions and, subsequently, a less constructive attitude on the part of the staff. Remember that an old, overcrowded mental hospital can depress the staff, just as it can the patients. One writer reported having to queue to see the psychiatrist, who then discussed his case with the charge-nurse as if he were not present. I know too, that *noise* – a very harmful form of pollution – has sometimes hindered a patient's well-being. Thus, our walk through the wood was symbolic of a retreat into a peace which is in the essence of spiritual healing. The Gospel narratives of the healings performed by Jesus so often speak of crowds, excitement and factors that created noise. One can well imagine the act of healing causing a great hush to fall upon the crowd, much as true religious experience can as easily cause a person or congregation to be still, as to create 'speaking in tongues' for example. In one of her books about the Wye Valley, her home from which she edited 'The Girls Own Paper', Flora Klickmann wrote of 'the presence on the hills'. It was in stillness, in peace, that she felt the awesome presence of the Creator. One may enter a quiet church or cathedral and gain the same 'healing presence', as it has been called. Ours is a world of noise, round-the-clock entertainment, portable radios, recorders, and television sets. Useful as these gifts are, do they help us to comprehend Creation, as, say, a walk in the woods? Voices in generations long past warned that men divorced from the *evident* unity of creation – in great cities, for example – would soon lose their reason for living.

We consider ourselves masters of creation, having conquered time and space. But, to the anxious, Jesus says 'gaze upon the flowers of the field' if you really want to understand the essence of real glory.

Well, such thoughts came to me often enough, as I wandered through the woods. One member of the staff, mistaking my ambling for a more energetic interest, suggested that I might ask the gardeners for a job.

'My interest,' I replied carefully, 'is more in the way things are. I do not feel that I have any right to disturb Mother Nature.' I paused. 'However, if you could ask the G.P.O. to come up and look at our useless telephone kiosk . . .' I suppose the psychiatrists regarded all this in the line of 'relaxation therapy' which was after all, the basis of the operation. One of the spare rooms at Harvey, quaintly called 'the Library', was empty of anything except an old desk on which stood the most ancient of typewriters. Few books were evident though a few small chairs, evidently designed for toddlers, were near at hand. I wondered if the Library was perhaps intended for someone who wished to produce a manuscript, and if I had stayed at the hospital longer, I might well have suggested a little essay competition. The typewriter looked rather like that ancient machine I possessed during the war, useful enough until my brother struck it with the family axe. Was that, I wondered, a commentary on my literary aspirations? It was, incidentally, in my early teens, when I first felt an urge to write, that I first became aware of my 'tin nerves'. It had taken a quarter of a century to get me into a mental hospital and, apparently, to resurrect the typewriter on which I had first bashed out pieces for the local paper.

The Library was used for relaxation sessions, in

which a useful tape recording on relaxation was played back to anyone feeling like doing the relevant exercises. I possessed a terrible guilt feeling about the tape recording, for sister, on at least one occasion, suggested that I listened to it and profited thereby. I listened to a little of the tape, but the exercises seemed too energetic for me, so I switched off the machine and took to the beloved woods instead. A squirrel apparently asleep on a branch seemed to have acquired the art of relaxation without any tape recording – but he, alas, was not talking to me.

6

A Short Trip to E.C.T.

You could have made a quip: 'Mr Hayes is in a daze'. A businessman in his early fifties, Mr Hayes did indeed seem in a daze when he arrived at the house. His speech was slurred, though one could understand him quite well. He shuffled across the room like an old man, and looked very, very tired. He was put to bed only an hour or so after he arrived, that afternoon in July, and I went into his room to take him some light refreshments – and, as I hoped, to cheer him up. It was obvious that he had been suffering considerable strain for months, even years, and had come to that point of 'stop' which our unconscious intelligence uses to over-rule our active egos.

He took the tea and cake gratefully, and I sat on the corner of the bed. Sister had given me permission to stay 'for a few minutes' so I used these to reassure the new patient.

'You might feel pretty low right now,' I said. 'Most of us do when we get in here. But you'll soon start to feel much better.'

'They're going to give me E.C.T.,' he mumbled. 'What's that?'

For a mere layman, it was no simple question. The E.C.T. unit was only just down the road, and some of the patients had this Electro-Convulsive Therapy regularly. One of the staff had explained to me that it was a simple matter of giving the brain a shock to break up (it was hoped) those thought patterns which caused long-term anxiety. The word 'convulsive' was a little frightening, but – because of the muscle relaxants given to the patient before treatment – such convulsions were more in the order of mild tremors, in the limbs, for example. Most of the patients with whom I discussed E.C.T. said things like, 'It leaves me with a headache, but I feel a lot better afterwards.' Thus, I gently explained to the bewildered Mr Hayes that it was a well-tried treatment that gave a mild electric shock to the brain, but, as one was usually unconscious when E.C.T. was given, there was no cause for apprehension.

Of all the cases in our house, Mr Hayes was the one that progressed quickest through E.C.T. and the helpful environment in which he now found himself. Indeed, as one of the patients put it, 'he seemed to lose ten years of his age within a week or two'. Certainly, from the somewhat dazed individual I had met that first night, he changed into a competent eager-to-learn individual. He confided to me that he was becoming worried about his business, since there was no-one to deputize for him.

'It's a problem,' I agreed. 'But look at it this way – no-one is indispensable in this life. Your stay here is at the present moment more important than anything else in your life.'

E.C.T. has received a bad press at times. It is like any other medical treatment – the best that we can do at this stage of knowledge. The mind/brain relationship is a mystery still, and the wisest psychiatrists are those who know *how little they know*. Like drug therapy, E.C.T. will work better with some patients than with others. Some may not benefit at all – or *believe* that they have received no benefit. One of the saddest cases was that of a fine young man – in his late thirties – who discharged himself, simply because he was so discouraged. Unfortunately, his family wanted him home, so that he *thought* that he had no reason for staying. All therapy is long-term, simply because mental illness springs from experiences often buried deep in the unconscious. E.C.T. tries to break up the 'attack-triggers' buried in the mind, to help the brain/mind function in a new way. It is a matter of short steps, one at a time. I sometimes think that every mental hospital should have this sign above its entrance portals: 'WE CANNOT PERFORM MIRACLES OVERNIGHT – BUT WE KNOW HOW YOU FEEL'. Another form of treatment is narcosis in which the patient is quite literally put to sleep for a week, two, three weeks. Apart from the important rest gained by the patient, this can help the subconscious mind to 'work out its own tensions'. The patient is awakened from time to time for a short, brief exercise or examination – there are no 'Sleeping Beauties' awaiting the arrival of a medically qualified Prince Charming. Here, again, the patient can believe that he/she is making little progress, because he feels no better. With the amazing progress in antibiotics, for example, we are used to rapid results in the treatment of diseases which disabled our grandparents for weeks. Somehow, modern man cannot bring himself to realize that there is no 'wonder cure' for the troubled mind. Over-zealous Christians who (somewhat unsympathetically at times) say that mental illness is due to 'unconfessed sins' might well remember that the Fall affected the whole man. Unconfessed sin may cause mental illness, but it is more likely to be a traumatic experience that is at the root of a patient's fear, expressed in agoraphobia, for example.

So I watched the little group of patients make their

way to the building in which they received their E.C.T. treatment. As they always arrived back at the house in good time for lunch, I gained the impression that the treatment itself was fairly short. Patients had differing views, and it was never wise to press them for answers so soon after treatment. Just occasionally, a depressed patient might say something like, 'I go, but I don't think it does me any good' but, on the whole, they were ready to co-operate with the doctors. The improvement in the condition of the patients usually spoke for itself. E.C.T. seemed reserved for patients whose condition was perhaps more serious than those like myself who were rational and in control of the situation, *apart from specific phobias*. One of our E.C.T. patients, Lucille, occasionally suffered terrible depression when she cried and threw objects across the room. Mr Hayes when he came into the hospital, was obviously 'at the end of himself' whilst other E.C.T. patients were middle-aged or old people who, for various reasons, could not be treated effectively by drugs. None of the treatment at the hospital was intended to change one's basic personality. Depression is an affliction, like sciatica or gout: one's inner self or spirit can recognize it as such. In serious cases, people tend to lose hope because they cannot believe that they will ever become 'better'. This lack of hope is one of the causes of suicide amongst people prone to depression, especially as these number people who are among the most creative or sensitive people in the population. When, recently, a well-known and respected television personality committed suicide, leaving a note stating 'I can stand it no longer', he was probably referring to some form of depression.

'Ah,' says the stout-hearted evangelical at this point. 'But the Lord's people need not be depressed. Neither need they bother with E.C.T., when they have recourse to prayer.'

Taken to an extreme logic, such a standpoint results in Christian Science or in the Jehovah's Witness attitude towards blood transfusions. Prayer is undoubtedly an important factor in the healing of the troubled mind, remembering that the patient may not, or perhaps, cannot pray during the course of his illness. The man who took up his bed and walked would never have been healed but for the persistence of his friends in getting him to Jesus.

Depression is noted in the Bible – the down-hearted Elijah, after his great victory at Carmel; Jonah beneath the wilting gourd; the two downcast disciples on their way to Emmaus, are a few that come to mind. God may give his people great victories, but they are never easy ones. I recall a preacher telling of his own experience of depression.

'I would walk up and down outside the church in which I was to preach,' he said, 'just trying to summon up enough courage and energy to go in.' This is not as unusual an experience for preachers as some congregations imagine, and it is really essential that the preacher – be he layman or minister – really senses the love of God at work in the church. When I poured out my heart to the psychiatrist, he gave me all his attention and sympathy. I can, alas, recall times when I have tried to reach scattered, inattentive congregations which did not seem to care whether or not the sermon was given. How we need uplifting! How we need love and vision at work in the local church!

The pentecostal have, of course, been among the most active in praying for the sick, and in this, the anxious and down-hearted are included. Whilst obviously sincere and following good scriptural example, some ministers have been unaware of the need to persist in the follow-up work. In some churches, the pastoral ministry – visiting with people in their homes – has almost disappeared, and it is hardly to be wondered at that members of such churches cease to pray. *The role of the minister in praying with the individual member is not to be forgotten.* This applies to all churches, all congregations, by the way.

As the author has himself experienced, one experiences something like an electric shock, or a great power of joy, during individual prayer in a church where ministers call for the sick or anxious to come forward. One wonders if this power is anything like the E.C.T. given in hospital. The experience called 'the baptism of the Holy Spirit' does not necessarily manifest itself identically in diverse situations or persons, but it should always leave an after-glow of grace, gratitude, love, a deepening of fellowship. It is true that someone who is mentally ill can be healed instantaneously through the intervention of the Holy Spirit, but we must not forget that life is something of a school for all of us.

Thus, my month in mental hospital – and the years of struggle with anxiety – have made me a person vulnerable enough to recognize my own need of love, and, more important, the needs of others. Christians are being called to be set apart in this sense, rather than in the negative attacks on tobacco, alcohol, even pornography. I dislike smoking intensely, and consider the pressures of alcohol advertising (on television, for instance) little less than a national disgrace. In mental hospital, one encounters the 'chain smoker' (as far as the rules permit) whose nicotine-stained fingers confess years of tension as clearly as his medical records. He may be only a few steps in experience away from that chapel steward who crushes out his cigarette when it is time to enter church for the service. We all have our own weaknesses, and I remember that dear man of Christ, Pastor Stanley Belcher putting it plainly enough, 'I don't talk much about banning alcohol. I know how hard it is for me to pass a second-hand bookshop.' But the pastor, like so many Christians of diverse experience, always tried to show that walking with Christ spoke for itself – or Himself. It is the truth that sets us free, not the observance of prohibitions: and that truth has a dynamism of its own.

It may be that hospital units small enough to create 'a therapeutic community' have more success with E.C.T., for example, than those large hospitals where one so easily becomes a number on a record card. Research has shown how a placebo – that is, a tablet with no active ingredients whatsoever – has had a beneficial effect on some patients, *simply because they trusted the doctor*. Treatment within mental hospitals is constantly undergoing revision, so that E.C.T. may one day be dropped in favour of a better method – when it is discovered. We cannot leave the influence of the Holy Spirit at the hospital gates. If the scriptures teach us at all, they show that Jesus recognized anxiety as a major factor in making men and women less than they were intended to be. Sometimes, I wondered how Jesus would speak to those patients with whom I shared my life. Young Lucille, for instance, or Bruce, or any of the others. And, in a strange way, I found myself caring for them, in a way which I had not cared for fellow church members, for example. Maybe that is what the Lord wanted to say to *me*.

7

The Mail Bag

Dr Hunter opened the bulky file. We met twice a week –
for about an hour – to talk about my job, family background, childhood, ideas, etc. Unlike one or two other
psychiatrists that I have met, he was not preoccupied by
sex as a possible cause of mental distress. Towards the
end of our meetings (probably about ten in all) he asked
me if I had learned anything during my sessions at the
hospital.

'I feel that I was trying to do too much,' I reflected,
'and that I was not giving enough time to my family. I
feel that my phobia is something I have to live with, but
that I recognize it for what it is.'

He nodded.

'Good,' he said. 'I had a very interesting chat with
your wife when she came last visiting day, and everything seems fine there. Our job here as psychiatrists is to
help you – the patient – find out what it is that is wrong
in your life. We're not able to heal anybody. That's not
what we're here for.'

'I think I had become stale,' I added. "Nothing in my
life seemed at all refreshing. Even my church life seemed
flat.'

'Many of us might say that the church was failing in
its mission,' he replied. 'But perhaps other people in
your church see things in the same way.'

My mail certainly underlined those words. Just
before entering the hospital, I had written an article for

'The Christian Record' and had described my own feelings, and the way in which the church might develop its ministries for the anxious. In the weeks that followed, Anne brought many letters into the hospital – mail from people who, having read my article, and written to me care of the newspaper. The good people at 'The Christian Record' had forwarded the mail to my home address. As, at the time of preparing this book, I have still to reply to all the mail I have received, it is hard to put it all into some kind of perspective. The letters fell into three major categories. Most were from people who had suffered mental illness and who were still coping with it in, or out of, hospital. Others were from people who had overcome anxiety and other mental ailments with the help of the church, local ministers and specialists working together. The smallest category came from people who offered encouragement and prayers. A minister asked if I had considered producing a leaflet that might be used in counselling and visitation. The tone of his letter suggested that he encountered mental/spiritual ailments frequently in his ministry. Looking at the letters from people who had been patients in hospital, I was impressed by the gratitude of most, and just the occasional sad note from one who had been 'shunted about' from ward to ward, or hospital to hospital. None of the letters really surprised me, for I had encountered people in similar situations long before I ever entered hospital myself. I shared some of the letters with a fellow church-member, a Methodist of the old school, a fine man whose opinion I respect. A year or two ago, he had faced a serious illness himself, and in a subtle way which had not perhaps been recognized by those closest to him, he had softened into a gentleness which commended his faith.

'You could write a book,' he suggested, smiling. 'You were just fortunate to have your breakdown when you did. Just think of all the interesting people that you met . . . and all the letters you'll have to answer . . .'

Strangely enough, I did not share any of the letters with my own psychiatric mentor, Dr Hunter. He might well have been amazed at *his* patient getting so much mail from patients of other doctors. But, in one of our group therapy sessions, he agreed that there was a real need of the small therapeutic group in the community. The pressures of modern society, planning of new towns and cities, television and other factors have created a greater 'social distance' between people. We even sit far apart at our church services. With the modern marketeer's emphasis on personal ownership, personal possession, personal success, the individuality of *the person* has been emphasized to the extent that we no longer feel that we are of one body of humanity. Looking at the accident rates on our over-crowded roads, who feels now, as John Donne, that the death bell rings not for the individual, but for all of us, for no man is an island? The philosophy of contemporary society is that all men are islands; we all stand alone for what we can get in terms of possessions, success, status. My hospital experience stood that philosophy on its head: the greatest of all, as Jesus said, is the servant of all. Not that Ken Wright and I felt especially good as we daily wheeled the meal trolley to the kitchens where (as far as I can recall) the making of chips always seemed in progress. You will find in most hospitals, men who have spent themselves physically and/or mentally in the service of some vast organization. Paternalistic as the organization may be, it has demanded too much. Thus, men of early middle-age have to make that hard decision: the purpose of their lives. It is to 'be successful' in monetary terms (and all that success means)? Or is it something simpler? In the years before us, group therapy in hospitals will be faced increasingly by these questions. As one American psychologist has remarked, 'When a senior executive decides to find a simpler life, I don't call it "dropping out". I call it "breaking through" – because he is breaking through to the life that will really satisfy him.'

We discussed this question fully in one of our group therapy sessions and finally decided that, in this present world, 'success' was far too dubious an asset. 'Contentment', for example within one's family, was to be preferred – a message more easily recognized by the young than by the old these days.

I had taken into hospital, in addition to several books (which remained unread) a large stock of stationery (unused) and postage stamps (unlicked). I did not receive many letters from friends, and decided that the stack that arrived from 'The Christian Record' article would have to wait until I arrived home. The hospital rules were very simple, and I kept them all – except one. I missed my radio, and arranged to have a small set sent in from the hi fi shop in which I worked. I pointed out that, as the hospital rules stated that radios were not permitted, the radio would have to be disguised as something else. You may imagine my surprise when a grinning porter handed me a square box labelled on all sides: 'This is definitely *not* a radio set'.

I may safely claim to have widened my abilities in other directions, and that thanks to Poppy. An attractive and very constructive woman, Poppy had a recurring ailment that took her into the mental hospital for a few weeks every year. As she was a qualified social worker and had done some nursing, Poppy did her very best to help the patients, and was always suggesting functions at the social centre. One night, she organized a most successful dance, and I was roped in as 'disc jockey'. I would have done it for no-one else, especially as, at the height of the evening, I was surrounded by weighty young men who insisted that I play all their records – made by 'way out' pop groups, and certainly insuitable for the waltz, foxtrot or veleta. Poppy managed to bring the best out in people, and in other circumstances, would have made an excellent psychiatrist herself (though the regimen might have been more hectic). With another patient, she helped arrange a collection for a gift to be presented to one of the nurses who was about to be married. A handsome set of sheets and pillow-cases were the result, and I will never forget the hap-piness on the patients' faces as the gift was presented to the young nurse. Naturally, I insisted that the young lady should make a speech! But she was almost speech-less . . .

It is so easy to get people to rely on the hospital', the sister said one day. 'That is why we get you home on weekends if we can.' Some people (just a few) had become 'hospitalized' to the extent that they were per-fectly happy to stay as patients, even going home at weekends, but they could not face life in any normal way. Some critics of hospital treatment seem to think that people are deliberately hospitalized as a source of cheap labour; in my experience, nothing could be further from the truth. I am sure that this is one reason why I was discharged so soon. I was settling in too well. I had improved in many ways, a good drug treatment had been established, and I was far more confident in my ability to travel, and to work. Nevertheless, when one Monday morning – exactly a month after my arrival – the head psychiatrist obliquely raised the matter of my going home, I was a little súrprised. I had expected a minimum hospitalization period of six weeks. But I had to be honest. I told him that, whilst very grateful for all the care I had received, I did not see how the hospital could help me further.

'Good,' he smiled. 'We'll see about your going home this week.'

In fact, I left the following morning, with a supply of drugs to 'tide me over' until I could report to my doctor, and with two very heavy cases containing mainly unread books, unused stationery and unworn clothes. There was the usual round of goodbyes, and then Poppy – generous as ever – drove me into town as far as the bus station. There was one final flourish. The charge nurse called me as I struggled out of the house.

'There's been a phone call for you,' he said. 'There's been an emergency at home. The toilet cistern has gone for a burton, so your wife will hang on at home for you.'

One of the nurses – a stout, coloured lady – collapsed with laughter.

'My, oh, my,' she said. 'Now ain't that enough to give anyone a breakdown?'

A few more of the patients left that week, though – even as I write some six weeks after my departure – some of the patients are still receiving treatment. One of the staff whispered to me that the doctors had decided to 'let me go' because I probably would have discharged myself if they had not beaten me to it. I did not believe that story. As I said, 'I was just settling down when they told me I could go.'

Ken Wright, standing at the door and smiling in his

characteristic way, said. 'Will you be looking in to help me with the meals trolley?'

Then, with a wave, Poppy and I drove off, around the pleasant, flower lined roads of the hospital and towards the entrance. I could hardly believe that this was the very same place I had seen through the dismal, rain-streaked windows of the taxi only a month earlier. But it was . . .

8

Re-Entry

The streets of the city were as busy as ever, choked by traffic, since we were in the peak of the holiday period. Poppy could only pause behind a large van, as the queue of traffic waited at a road interchange. I clambered from her car, and, with a brief 'Goodbye' gained the comparative tranquillity of the pavement. How different everything looked! Or perhaps the change was in me . . . the clamour around me seemed like a film, unreal. I picked up my suitcase, and walked to the bus station, a somewhat dingy place. Once, I met some meths drinkers who had virtually taken over the Gents Toilet and it was not uncommon to see some 'derelict' looking for what our American friends call 'a handout'. Many of these people suffer from some kind of mental illness, but somehow have fallen through our 'Welfare State net'. Organizations like the East End Mission of the Methodist Church, Samaritans and Salvationists are only too well aware of the growth of mental illness in Britain. As for me, I had my drugs – Anafranil, an antidepressant and Librium, a tranquillizer – to keep me going for those months necessary for a recovery. One could not hope to overcome a twenty-year old phobia in a few weeks. However, as I took that first bus trip home alone, after my weeks in hospital, it was a kind of triumphant re-entry into the world. I could manage that, at least. When I arrived home, I found the diligent plumber cementing a joint in the external waste pipe. At once, he told me of the extent of the job:

'Hadn't been done properly last time', he said sadly. 'People don't take the trouble these days.'

As I paid him for his services, I mentioned that I had just arrived home from hospital. Remembering our group therapy discussion on prejudice, however, I did not mention that it had been the local *mental* hospital.

'Nice to be home again,' he smiled. Yes, especially when the plumber has fixed things, I reflected. He departed, and I walked into the garden. Had I really been away for a whole month? The experience at hospital was already gaining a dream-like quality. However, a few days later, various papers came through the post to remind me that all had been reality. I was now an outpatient at the infirmary and had to report for an interview a week or two later. That first interview impressed me considerably. It was held inside the shining new wing of the hospital, in a special Psychiatric Centre on the fifth floor. Wandering through the beautifully decorated, thickly carpeted corridors to the lift, I realized that this, too, was an achievement. There had been a time when merely to enter a large building, even a restaurant, would bring on a sense of panic. A Christian working for one of the well-known national charities confided that he, too, had faced the same problem during his work.

'I think, perhaps, people gave me money for the charity because I looked – and felt – so ill', he said. That was five years ago. I wonder if he, too, finished up in a mental hospital, or if he struggles on . . . or if the Lord has, in some way, delivered him. When I arrived at the Psychiatric Centre, I felt a little depressed, and sat near the door. The place was crowded, and the patients covered a wide age-range, teenagers to old age pensioners. When one reflected that this was just *one* clinic, on *one* day, in *one* hospital . . . My meditation was interrupted by the arrival of my psychiatrist, one of three or four on duty that day. As my papers had not yet arrived from the mental hospital, we had a talk about my present situation. I explained that I had returned to the hi fi store, where I had worked as a senior salesman. It was not an easy job, since customers seemed so easily annoyed about delays in obtaining spares or equipment, but – for a Christian – there were compensations. On the previous day, an elderly lady had come in to thank me for the delivery of a radiogram arranged by me.

'It was for my husband,' she explained. 'He doesn't have long to live, because he has a serious heart condition. So I thought I would buy him that radiogram because he always wanted one.'

The lady went on to explain that her doctor had suggested that she enter mental hospital (the one, indeed, I had attended) for an unspecified illness.

'But how can I go?' she asked me. 'I have my husband to look after.'

There were no other customers in the shop, so I took time to speak to her.

'Remember this,' I said. 'When your husband has gone to be with the Lord, go into mental hospital. You will need to be looked after yourself with all the added strain you have gone through.'

I told her a little of my own experience in the hospital, and I urged her to go to her doctor, when her husband had died, so that she could be given a place in the hospital.

'I am so grateful for your talking to me,' she said. 'You get so lonely sometimes.'

Only a few days later, another customer mentioned

some of his problems to me. Thieves had stolen his colour television set and audio equipment, and, in addition, done much damage to his house. His wife was in hospital, with arthritis, so he had plenty on his mind. He had entered the store to look at some inexpensive audio systems, presumably to choose one for his wife when she returned home, so I showed him around and gave him several leaflets.

'What amazes me, is the way that your friends ignore you completely when some tragedy happens to you,' he said. 'They look the other way when they see me, as if having a robbery in your home was catching, like a disease.'

'Life will get better for you,' I said. 'I have been in hospital myself, and in the end, all that matters is what you are, yourself – the faith you have in yourself, and the faith you have in God.'

It is not easy to talk to anyone in such a way, when working in a shop, nor is it always advisable, but, since leaving hospital, I find that my attitude to other people has changed. I feel more open, more vulnerable. But then, no one was more vulnerable than Jesus, as far as other people were concerned. I had started back at work within a few days of leaving the hospital, perhaps making the return to routine too soon. The store was being reorganized, so I had my share of lifting and carrying to do. I did not tell the manager that the drug therapy, to which I was now committed, made my legs feel slightly weak at times. Being on one's feet most of the day was not perhaps the best way of life for someone like myself – but I persevered. As I gave away my car a year or two ago, and am now dependent upon public transport (a half hourly bus service that sometimes gets caught in the traffic jams) I found my working day quite a long one. I arrived home at about seven in the evening, and was ready to go to bed only an hour or two later. However, after over-working (or being *over-active* – there is a difference) for so many years, I could hardly protest. I did feel lonely on the buses, however, and felt that I wanted to share my experience with others. But the passengers were wrapped in their own pre-occupations – young girls giggling about some nonsense, women chatting about 'the price of things', men reading the paper. I had to wait for my second visit to the Out-patients Department for anything resembling a re-union.

It was one of those days full of surprises – I think that the Good Lord lays them on specially for me, as they come quite frequently. As I ambled along to the new wing of the hospital, I heard a car horn and a familiar voice: 'David.' It was Poppy, in her grey Austin, at the traffic lights. I leaped through the traffic, and into the car, just in time, as the lights turned to green. I ex-plained that I had twenty minutes to spare before I re-turned to the splendid Psychiatric Centre. Poppy, her usual cheerful self, was full of news. She told me that she had to return to the mental hospital for special in-jections, and that she thought that everyone there was so wonderful. One of our patient friends had discharged herself and seemingly disappeared – sad news, for people so disorientated can lapse into desperation, even suicide. In such cases, one can only pray, and hope. Poppy added that she was off for a holiday – as much for her overworked husband as for herself – and that she would contact me on her return from Europe. She drove me back to the hospital en-trance, and, with a final wave, disappeared in the heavy stream of traffic. Poppy . . . the salt of the earth. When a natural pessimist like me despairs of the human race, it is good to remember people like Poppy whose nature is to be kind and always cheerful. Truly, she was one of the most remarkable people that I had met up to that point in my passage through life.

I ambled along the carpeted corridors, then took the lift to the fifth floor. The helpful lady in the Psychiatric Centre was a little worried because I had not been 'officially registered' as a patient.

'Well, I'm here,' I said. 'Or nearly all here.'

I sat near the door whilst the good lady shuffled through some files and made various telephone calls. Then, to my joy and amazement, my good friend, Ken Wright, entered.

'You're not here to push the meals trolley,' I joked, referring to our adventures at the hospital. He laughed, and, after seeing the receptionist, took the seat next to mine. Looking fit and jovial, one would never suspect that he had so recently suffered a serious breakdown. He had returned to work, where he was very busy. A passing thought came into my mind: *too busy?* Companies tend to demand much from their executives, and he had retured to work even faster than I had. I believe that his period of convalescence was less than a week, but I may be mistaken. As we talked, Jennie entered. Jennie, a nineteen-year-old, had been in mental hospital, too, but hers had been for the third time, and she was still in a nervous state. Her hands were trembling, and she looked as though she might burst into tears. We said 'hello' at once – there is a real fraternity between former patients at the hospital – and she sat with us. As my interview was due, I suggested that Jennie and I might have a coffee together later, though this did wreck my plans for a rare trip to the cinema. My own psychiatrist, a sympathetic lady, suggested that I continue the drug therapy. In retrospect, I realize that I have been able to speak easily to all the psychiatrists at the hospital, though I had some proper awe for the 'head man'. I mention this, because the strain suffered by nursing and medical staff is sometimes overlooked. The psychiatrist mentioned that she had been a friend of a local doctor who had committed suicide only the week previously. Although the meeting with the psychiatrist was quite brief – about fifteen minutes – it did represent an important link with the hospital.

'I want to keep going forward, even though I feel nervous at times,' I said. 'I don't want to go into hospital again.' I was now thinking of all those who needed the all-too-limited facilities for the mentally ill in this country.

Jennie and I walked along to a nearby restaurant where we had coffee. To be precise, I had grape-fruit juice. As we talked, Jennie seemed to be more relaxed, and told me that she had been offered a job.

'But I may have to go back into hospital, because I can't sleep,' she said.

Although it is always a temptation (for Christians, especially) to over simplify any situation, it seemed that Jennie shared that same hang-up: lack of confidence.

'One thing I learned in hospital is that we just have to cope with one day at a time.' I said. 'I'm not very good at practising it, but I think that, if we just try, the job has to be secondary. What really matters is that precious person that is *you*. The hospital can't ever *cure* anyone with our kind of problem, but it can help us understand how to cope. It's never easy.'

We left the restaurant, and walked along the high road overlooking the city. A gentle wind blew against our faces, and, as our ways parted, I said to Jennie, 'Remember that you are loved. Your fiance loves you. Your parents love you. I love you. Above all, God loves you. I don't know what your religious belief is, but remember that God is love. If we but knew it, we are surrounded by love.'

I almost wondered where the words came from – they were certainly spontaneous. I watched Jennie walk away, down into the crowded city.

I wondered if perhaps I should consider entering mental nursing, or some similar job. After all, I had gained a social science diploma, all those years ago, but had never succeeded in persuading anyone to let me use it professionally. I wrote a letter to the hospital, but the Matron replied that it was never wise to appoint patients to the staff. That, I suppose, was that. In the meantime, people write to me on these matters, and this book will provoke a further mail-bag. Everywhere, people are waiting to be touched by reassurance and an emphasis on God's Love at work in this mixed-up world. You do not require any diploma to tell people about *that*. A week or two after leaving hospital, I was asked to talk to a church group about my experiences and the meeting went on for almost 1½ hours, because there were so many questions. It seems that mental illness – and the need of love at work in our communities – have become so evident that the local church is recapturing its priorities. And, to those who inquire if I am cured or merely temporarily eccentric, I would say that, having suffered my first attack of agoraphobia when I was a mere fifteen or sixteen, it took a quarter of a century to get me to that place of assurance. For, whatever happens now, I know that there is a help to be obtained, that even the most spiritually-minded person may need psychiatric help some time. The good psychiatrist offers insights. He is not a substitute for faith, but will help the sick mind to recover through those healing instincts that are within all of us. If I am an evangelical at all, it is in this matter: the lady with the radiogram, for example, is the kind of person I gladly counsel now. Definitions are hard to find, of course, for churchgoers are not always good at pastoral care and visitation. Sometimes, the absent churchgoer may feel it is a matter of 'out of pew, out of mind'. We rarely used that overworked word, 'God', in our group therapy sessions, but it was quite impossible to leave Him out of our considerations. Whenever we tried to help one another through the spiritual deeps, we were sharing in a ministry. The sister called it 'a therapeutic community'; some might say it was most akin to the church as it ought to be in this age of turmoil.

To Christians who are going through the difficulties that I suffered for so long, I would say that God moves in mysterious ways to make us the kind of people we should be. If you ask me to define my experience, I would say it was a lesson in humility, just as it proved to be an unusual and uplifting exercise of faith. But remember that it started on a wet Monday morning, when this writer would willingly have hid his head under the blankets. It was just that I found a new meaning of that word 'love' as I met others making their own uncertain and sometimes hard way through this journey we call life.

The Earth and the Fullness Thereof

I had completed this little book, and the manuscript was slumbering on my desk, awaiting despatch to the publishers, when I faced a crisis that might well have provoked a further collapse. I lost my job at the hi fi store.

It was inevitable parting of the ways, in one sense. I had told the manager, earlier in the year, that it would be wise for him to find a replacement. At the time, my wife was bringing me into town every day (my 'nerves' would not permit me to make the journey alone). However, I did not realize that I would have to go into hospital so quickly. The store manager was kind enough to take me back again when I came out from hospital, but 'things did not work out'. Perhaps he did not appreciate the 'woozy' effect of the drugs, and there was some disagreement about holiday pay. At all events, I had to face that difficult task of finding new employment within a week or two of leaving hospital. Registering at the Department of Employment (which I found most helpful and sympathetic, by the way), writing job applications, completing job application forms, attending interviews – all these tasks inherent in job hunting can be a strain at the best of times. My psychiatrist smiled when I told her the news that I was unemployed.

'Oh, you'll find something to suit you,' she smiled. Strangely enough, I took a part-time job in a department store – and was offered a permanent position my very first day as 'temporary'. I have now learned to trust the Lord more in this matter of employment. Looking back at the various jobs I have held in my life, I can see how endogenous depression, undiagnosed until last year, has haunted my life. Furthermore, I seem to move in a new dimension now, able to appreciate the needs of others. Comparative strangers – like other employees in the department store – tell me about their friends and relations who have suffered, or are suffering, a nervous breakdown. All the same, I will have to take my telephone number out of the local directory now, since I am recognized as someone with a ready ear, 'someone who understands'.

The department store job has been good for me, and, as if by jovial providence, many former friends have 'popped in', most of them amused and amazed to see me behind a counter. Only a week or so ago, Jennie came in, trembling but looking much better than she had that day I met her in the outpatients department. She told me that a doctor had taken her into his home for a couple of months, given her a room of her own and invited her to be 'a member of the family'. The therapy had obviously proved of great benefit, since Jennie was holding a part-time secretarial job. She was still taking various drugs on prescription, but the extent of her victory, in staying out of mental hospital this time, was to be admired. I took one of her shaking hands in mine.

'I have this trouble sometimes,' I smiled. 'But it's getting better.'

As she was nervous of going into the store lift alone, I took her to the third floor, where she planned to buy some clothes. As I watched her cross the floor, I could not help but think that this indeed is the stuff of which miracles are made. A small triumph, the care of a doctor and his family, a part time secretarial job, the kindness of one's friends and family . . .

A week or so later, a friend of mine holding an important management job in a large company was told that his position was being 'phased out'. That this news was a shock was obvious from his pale appearance. I wondered if this news would have any effect upon him: within a few days, he was ill in bed, with a 'flare-up' of a latent kidney complaint. Coincidence? Someone within our own family had a two-month illness after he was found redundant (and that after his employers had persuaded him to move across the country to take up promotion). Family physicians are being faced increasingly with this kind of illness, whilst suicide – in extreme cases – is not so much the balance of mind disturbed, as the balance of environment destroyed.

My friend will probably have to take some kind of demotion. But, like many others in his situation, he wonders if he should look for some kind of independence from what is sometimes called 'the rat race'. Certainly, many young people are trying to define success anew, as some kind of spiritual fulfilment rather than worldly achievement. In that, the churches have a great opportunity to speak to today's young idealists.

Another lesson of the past few months – my post-hospital life – is that God moves in a mysterious way, but He moves nevertheless. The secret of a successful personal ministry today is that kind of open, projected love that some call prayer. Do not be afraid of loving people – and showing it. Perhaps the most important lesson of all is that the Lord works in the commonplace. Recently, I talked with a lady who is responsible for arranging typing and secretarial courses for mental hospital patients – especially young women who need to prepare for some kind of employment.

'We never hurry them. We try to give them

confidence in their work. When they have found that confidence, they will soon build up their typing speed. We try to give them a skill of which they can be proud.'

It seems such a little thing: a word to a neighbour, a ride in the lift with someone too nervous to take it alone, a sympathetic word during a typing lesson. But of such moments is therapy shaped, and personal relationships transformed. Of course, theological discussion can define this or that activity of God in less troublesome ways. In that matter of heaven for example, I find that proof texts help me less than the certainty that God is Love. And, if God is Love, He is wherever Love is. I find that my life has been enriched and perhaps saved by a multitude of good men and women who sometimes wore the badge of Christianity and who sometimes did not.

But they exhibited a kind of love that I cannot forget. The urge towards permissiveness and the sale of pornography may have much to do with hunger for real human relationships, for commercialized sex is recognized as second-best even by its purveyors.

To those who despair this morning or who retreat from life this afternoon, I can only say that the fundamental reality for me is the Love of God. No wonder that the Lord had to select Paul for the task of instructing the church, for only a man of such verbal power and intellect could begin to describe the love of God, though he spoke with the tongues of men and of angels. Life is too short for any Christian to be less than Christ-like. God is too great for any of us finally to conclude that we count for nothing. We inherit, within our spirit, the earth and the fullness thereof.

About Agoraphobia

The extent of agoraphobia – fear of open spaces, and/or of leaving the home – is widespread in Britain, and affects at least 500,000 people. A phobia is an exaggerated fear, for example one may be legitimately afraid of leaving one's home during a thunderstorm, *but to be afraid of leaving the home at any time* is irrational.

Because such phobias are very difficult to treat, busy doctors have tended to prescribe tranquillizers and/or mood elevators, and the now-notorious amphetamines were widely prescribed for depression and associated ailments in the early 1960s. Only in recent years, has the medical profession taken agoraphobia seriously, but little is known about it, and arguments about treatment continue. The philosophy at the hospital I attended was that of giving the patient 'relaxation therapy' and helping him to organize his/her life within the limitations of the ailment. Indeed, the head psychiatrist – a man whose wisdom I would not question – talked about giving my own phobia 'a hard knock'. The word 'cure' is rarely used in mental illness, although (as I saw) great improvements in the patient's condition may be obtained. I would encourage anyone who has fought anxiety symptoms for a long time to seriously consider a period in a mental hospital, though you may have to press this point upon your doctor, who has due regard to the stretched facilities at many hospitals.

The phrase 'anxiety state' is often used in association with agoraphobia, and can mean virtually any situation in which the patient over re-acts to external stimuli. It is sensible and natural to feel fear when you are in a field and suddenly notice a bull. The body instinctively acts to make you run away. The anxiety state patient may get a sense of fear (or 'sudden panic' as it may be called) at any time and any where – climbing the stairs at home, in a restaurant (I can recall many meals ordered but left untouched!) or in a train or bus. In serious cases – as I noted among my neighbours when I lived in a Midlands town – young people can become so anxious that they will not leave their house for any reason. Even today, it is said that many people suffering from agoraphobia are not helped because they cannot even contemplate a journey to the hospital out-patients' department or psychiatrist's consulting rooms. I managed my consultation only because I was accompanied by my wife. Indeed, when the psychiatrist remarked that I was looking cheerful, I told him that I had at least managed to get to his rooms (no small victory in my condition).

'The Open Door' is an organization which tries to help the growing number of people suffering from this disconcerting ailment, and popular newspapers and magazines have recently printed articles about agoraphobia itself. 'Young Phobics' is a similar organization designed to help young people suffering from this ailment. In one sense, these are more accurate descriptions of a malady sometimes called 'nervous breakdown' (as one psychiatrist remarked, 'Show me the nerve that broke down'). Basically, the ailment seems to be a response of the inner self, the psyche, to an intolerable situation – too much pressure at work, a tragedy at home, uncertainty about buying a house, etc. Society is increasingly creating these 'crisis points' at which a breakdown occurs, and this is certainly one reason why many young people find themselves in mental wards.

The local church's role in this situation could be very important, in the sense that every community needs some kind of 'open house' in which help can always be found, even if this is a 'first stage of sympathy' before the social worker is brought in. For generations now, Christians and churches have become decreasingly available. It was the great Samuel Chadwick who said, many years ago, that it was a shame that so many churches opened their doors for no more than a few hours a week. Ministers have so many responsibilities these days that pastoral visitation has taken low priority, so that (as I have seen) people within church congregations can have deep spiritual problems but have no opportunity to discuss them with the minister. We are getting to the point where every church needs to be 'open' in one sense or another, to people who are in despair. Churches should sponsor 'small group' therapy activities. Indeed, it was the inspiration of John Wesley that he saw the class meeting as an extended family. Early Methodism was far more effective in this respect than the Methodist Church of today (of whom I am one) – not that this is any condemnation of the good Methodists in this generation. It is merely that we have become hypnotized by big answers to big questions (the role of the church, unity, inter-communion, etc) without realizing that the man next door needs a few answers to his questions *urgently*. Our society is creating many mental casualties. With young people experimenting with drugs, sex, the occult, way-out religions, we may well see a generation emotionally burned out by the time its members are twenty-five or thirty years of age. What, then, will be our message? It can be no less than the Gospel that saves the whole man, mind as well as soul,

intellect as well as spirit. I sometimes think that if the
churches of Britain were to preach the love of God con-
sistently for three months, we would see a great revival.
For man finds significance in his own life as he finds
meaning in the universe. Fear springs from a sense that
we are somehow alone. Jesus said that perfect *love* casts
out fear: not good works, or speaking in tongues, or
works of evangelism, important as these are in their
place. Perfect love: can we practice it? We may attain to
it, and in preaching it afresh, heal the broken minds of
our age.

Why Christians Crack Up

(This article featured in the Church of England News-paper, Christian Record, and British Weekly issues dated June 30, 1972. It resulted in a large volume of correspondence including a letter from Lutterworth Press which led to this book.)

By the time this reaches the editor's well-stacked desk, I will be in a mental hospital. For how long, I'm not sure. Some weeks, at the very least. I am just one of those many Christians who 'crack up'. Indeed, during recent weeks when I have myself been feeling almost at the end of myself, I have been involved in helping one or two others who have appeared on my doorstep in varying degrees of anxiety.

In a way, I regard my retreat into a mental hospital as the Lord's good intention to 'get me away from the battle' for a while. I am drafting this article – one of the last acts before I pack my suitcase – because I want to raise this issue of mental health and the Church, so crucial to our times.

It is quite surprising how often hard-working minis-ters and church-workers suffer a collapse of the psyche, alternatively called 'overwork', 'anxiety state', 'acute stress', 'agoraphobia', 'nervous breakdown', and so on.

So many Christians seem to act as if such visitations are caused by a lack of faith or being out of the Lord's will – the latter being an especially glib view from one who has never had to walk through this particular valley. Others are baffled.

I don't think that I know of more than one or two churches who really understand what is involved in the healing of the spirit. And I can think of many who create situations that cause stress. So, to the causes . . . beware in case you recognize yourself!

Many ministers are greatly overworked. I had hoped to have a visit from my minister last week, when I was feeling rather low and wanted to discuss some matters with him. He didn't arrive. Poor man, he was involved with a bereavement which had itself caused a nervous breakdown within a family, and had all the other duties of running a number of churches.

Because we expect ministers to do far too much, we create something akin to a train which eludes him with ever-gathering speed, whilst church members feel isolated, because the minister cannot visit them often. Because we expect ministers to do far too much, we create stress situations twice over.

It is true that some churches very sensibly, have organized street-warden schemes, in which members agree to supervise streets or areas, reporting cases of illness or bereavement at once to the minister or church social worker. But such activities are only the beginning of the church's ministry.

The average church service so often misses out on the creating of that environment of love that really helps people to feel that they are loved. Our congregations are so often scattered and aloof, conscientiously attending services that are more like a formal lecture than a family reunion, as far as actual spiritual atmosphere is concerned.

And because the Sunday service is so often the only

time when members meet now, its very formality is not conducive to the confession of fears and faults, one to another.

I think we would be surprised if we knew just how many private fears and worries are carried in the average congregation, people who are slowly sinking spiritually, who clutch at church attendance like a man grasping a floating piece of timber as he goes down for the third time.

Another factor in all this is that the ethos 'Let Jack do it' prevails so often in Christian circles. When work looms on the horizon, so many opt for the willing horse. It is better to get tired *in* Christian work than to get tired *of* it, but the fact that we have so many good people who come to church and do nothing more (in the matter of sharing their spiritual gifts, for example) suggests that some *are* tired *of* it, before they have ever been involved *in* it.

In these days, when so many spiritual castaways walk this land (as you will certainly discover if you are identified as someone with a ready ear) every Christian needs to be able to pray with another person, to help another person be reconciled with God, to gain fresh heart from the Gospel. Every Christian needs to be able to speak in humility and joy to someone else facing deep personal problems. And, in the matter of mental illness, every Christian needs to identify with the one who is suffering.

Remember, a simple act of caring is often better than all the home spun wisdom on psychiatric illness. It seems to me more and more important that the church returns to its basic: see how these people love one another – still the best communications policy in the world.

As a Christian writer (of sorts!) I know the special loneliness experienced by anyone in a 'creative ministry'. Yes, there are moments when the Lord seems very near, and we gain much encouragement, but the 'Hallelujah Good Time' aspect of today's Jesus Movement misses out on the cross.

Jesus did not always live spiritually way above the lot of man; He came down from the Mount of Transfiguration to encounter disbelief, hatred, and finally death. I believe that preaching on these essential themes of Jesus' identification with us in depression, despair and seeming defeat can help the anguished soul.

In the end, the fact of the resurrection may be (as Paul so clearly perceived in his letter to the Corinthians) the only piece of spiritual reality to which the 'cracked-up Christian' can cling.

It is true, as the old hymn says, that when we meet at the foot of the Cross, we realize that we are all weak – even those of us who consider ourselves strong – and that the transfiguring power of the Cross is that which we need.

That could perhaps be our theme: *Transfiguration not Tranquillizers*. By tranquillizers, I also mean the tranquil homilies that sometimes pass as preaching these days.

The extent of mental illness in Britain is vast, and growing all the time. At least a quarter of a million people suffer from agoraphobia (as has this writer) defined as the 'dread of going outdoors'.

Anxiety can take many forms: the fear of entering buildings, cars, trains, buses. I have known only too well the sensation of dread on having entered a restaurant and ordered a meal, which I have been unable to eat.

A local preacher friend of mine mentioned that he used to walk up and down outside the church, in which he was to preach, trying to find enough courage to go within. Suppose the congregation had *loved* him, instead of merely listened to him. Ah, yes, we return to essentials again.

As I have finally reached the point, after many years' fight with this illness (for such it is, going back to fears of childhood, evacuation, etc.) that I cannot work – at least for the time being – I will perhaps get some new perspective. So, if any readers wish to write and share their own problems, I will do my best to answer all letters enclosing a stamped addressed envelope (preferably).

It would take a series of articles, not merely one, to look at this problem, and the way in which the church's ministries need to be developed. We need not so much stronger-than-thou counsellors, having taken a crash course (these may be useful sometimes) as churches filled with love reflected in a desire to share all things – the work, for example, the ministry and ministries, everyone's 'hang-ups' and the joy of just being a Christian.

I have met an amazing number of people with these mental illnesses. I even heard of one lady suffering from stress who was told to stay away from church until she could face it again – rather like facing a dental appointment! Shouldn't our ministry shine most in these situations? Shouldn't we have in those defeats, a spirit of victory which is the best possible medicine?

Mental illness does not disappear overnight, nor is it an expression of sin or lack of faith. It is an expression of the environment we have created for mankind, and of our humanity.

As I pack my bags for my stay in a mental hospital, I wonder if it would have been necessary if – instead of a willing horse – I had been one of a team. Well, that's the question that faces every Christian worker sooner or later. The Lord will have us rest sooner or later, even if it does take a nervous breakdown to do it.

GOD IN WARD 12

Richard Bewes

Richard Bewes, one of Britain's best known convention speakers and preachers has a regular ministry few know about.

As part of the work of his own Church he has developed a unique relationship with the local hospital. In addition to all the things a hospital chaplain would do he acts as disc jockey to a Christian music programme on the hospital radio and also presents a regular religious programme featuring members of his church. His bed by bed ministry is linked to what the patients are hearing over their headphones.

In this often amusing and sometimes moving little book, Richard describes the people he has met in hospital, their problems, fears, arguments and insights. He writes helpfully about the Christian understanding of healing and straightens out some of the strange ideas that get put about on the subject.

Above all it's just about as readable and enjoyable a book as you could find.

THE HOLY SPIRIT EXPERIENCE
Roger Salisbury

One of the key issues amongst Christians today is how someone receives and experiences the Holy Spirit. The Charismatic movement throughout the world is highlighting the long forgotten role of the Holy Spirit in lives of Christians and reports of people exercising 'the gifts of the Spirit' within the mainstream denominations are now commonplace.

But with these developments there has come controversy and reports of people being distressed over the teachings of some groups about 'Baptism in the Holy Spirit', 'the gift of tongues' and other related matters.

Roger Salisbury has written a lucid and simple outline of the Biblical teaching about the experience of the Holy Spirit in which he reluctantly finds himself taking issue not only with some of the teachings associated with the Charismatic movement, but also some of the views he once held.